MW01047463

ISBN:978-1-7368073-0-9

**Keep Breathing**

        **Breathe**

               **Breathe Mecka !!!**

# Table of Contents

**Dose 2**

# Second Call

To know Noah is to love him, born prematurely very thin in figure but with a mighty heart. Noah faced many challenges growing up, his biggest challenges was simple to most of us but was a daily fight for him, to breathe. Breathing, trouble breathing was something that he could not understand, why he couldn't play as other kids played. Despite what the doctor spoke on him he continue to push through even though he was already told he was defeated and wouldn't live pass six months.

Early, Noah had to be a strong, determined, and fighting young boy who also had to play the role of the man, father, big brother and little big brother. He did it with such pride, joy, loyalty, and honor. I remember my mom dressing us up with the same clothes on, but my white shirt had flowers in it and his shirt will be plain white. Matching jeans with dark blue jean down the side and light blue jean in the middle. We were going to take pictures at Clay Street, I remember my mother turning around and saying really Noah. He had peed himself, remind you he had been telling our mom he had to use the bathroom.

The picture guy was running behind, she didn't want to miss the appointment, or she would have to reschedule. So, we took the pictures with him with wet pants. We took one's sitting down first, then standing with Garfield behind us and I remember him just smiling and cheesing. A day I remember often, memories that come to me from basically looking at a picture.

Noah and I attended Barclay elementary school, where most of our family also went on our mother side. Incredibly determined to be and have a normal childhood he joined the basketball team, which he soon finds out he loves the sport except when he had to take breaks. I used to joke him, I believe he loved the sport because he see all the girls on the side lines screaming and yelling his name. He went from being fragile to the man of the hour, lol.

Going in and out of the hospital for asthma treatments after asthma attacks, I never saw his spirit break. Each time he sat there on the hospital bed, legs swinging from the edge, mask on his high yellow bright-eyed face and breathing machine going. Not long after the second or third treatment, he would be jumping and jittery from the medicine. My mother was like Noah sit down and I'm thinking how? How can he sit down? When that medicine got him going like that? Noah knew that for him to get back to his siblings, his friends, and his cousins he had to take those treatments and he did. One I will always cherish about those moments is when he put the mask on his face and he would look at me over the top of it, like oh boy (rolling his eyes) like here we go again.

After Grandma past, I begin to see a change in Noah overall attitude. We all used to walk cheerfully from home to school and after school to Grandma and PopPop house. He begins to hang out with more boys from the neighborhood, learning his way around the crazy streets of Baltimore from east, west, north and south. He never came to grips with how his, our lives had changed once losing Grandma. We went from structure, getting up at a certain time in the morning, eating breakfast, getting dressed for school and getting a snack, completing homework, eating dinner, bathing and getting ready for bed at night. Now we could come and go as we pleased, most times we made sure the other ate. I watched as he struggled with uncles coming to discipline him but never there to encourage him when he was on the right track. He also was the person to bare many secrets, mainly for his uncles and friends. Strangely when he could use it to his gain he did, lol with Jackie. Instead of talking about what was bothering Noah, he would take it out on anyone he had to fight physically. Prayer was something that came easy for me not so much for Noah, he didn't believe especially because of Grandma. I would try to get him to understand what I believe Grandma was trying to get us to truly understand about the love of God. Us needing and wanting things, he took things in his own hands, his rage became more intense specifically because our father was not being the man he once knew his father to be and getting high in front of our friends, now with no care of how it made us feel.

We were in the kitchen playing games, laughing, and eating when Josh, my godson, came up the steps from the man cave.

"Noah got shot," he said. We all stopped!

I said, "When and where?"

Josh said, "On Greenmount. He good though! He's on the way to the hospital."

We tried to continue to enjoy our Friday; however, you could see on our faces that we were worried. Josh came back up and talked to Edward off in the living room. They both came back in the kitchen to tell me, "He's gone."

I screamed, cried, and yelled so loud. It was so unexpected, especially because as far as I knew, he was not in the streets. I asked, "What happened?"

"Still waiting. Supposedly Noah was squashing an altercation that had happened while he was at work," Josh said, with tears falling from his face.

**Taking pictures brought me some peace....**

# Backstory

I talked to my brother Derrick and my cousin Jermaine, who were both in jail, to confirm that Noah was killed protecting Jermaine's younger brother, Cameron. Jermaine is the oldest son of my mother's sister, Donna, and at one point he was my favorite male cousin. We were always told who the gunman was; however, he was not in custody, nor was street violence returned. The story was, while Noah was at work, Cameron went into the boy's pockets for seventy dollars and took his cell phone.

When Noah got home from work, they had told him what had happened. Noah reached out to the boy and they met on Lorraine Avenue, two blocks from where he shared a row house with his siblings and mom before going away to prison for ten years. They all walked down toward Lorraine Avenue. Steven was in front of Noah. Steven is the grandson of my mother's brother, Shawn, and the son of his daughter, Sammy. Steven is the youngest of the cousins on my mother's side who were outside that night. Cameron and Jackson were behind Noah, and they all walked toward Lorraine Avenue.

Jackson is the youngest son of my mother's sister, Patricia. He is the true definition of a momma's boy, and he wants to be down so bad. Jackson was sheltered; he did no wrong in his mother's eyes. Most of the time when adults weren't around, Noah, Jermaine, and I would get him back for getting us in trouble. Now Noah gave the boy back the money and cell phone Cameron had taken. They shook hands. There were two other guys standing there with the guy who shot Noah.

Once Noah turned his back, one of the other guys gave a head nod and the gunman started shooting. They all ran. Noah was taking bullets to the back but still running. It was not until he tripped off the curb and fell that the guy came and stood over my brother (who could not see him), emptied the clip into him, and then walked back down the block.

I wanted to see if I could identify anyone who was out there the night my brother was shot; I reached out to homicide and asked if I could see the evidence they had. I wanted to watch the surveillance cameras, one of which they did not see at first because it was on the side of the Mayflower building. Not one of them, Jackson, Steven, or Cameron—all first cousins or friends—helped Noah. He died alone, gasping for air in the gutter. That was heart wrenching; I will never forget that image. All I could think was, *Where were my nephews when this happened?*

I was told he had the boys with him that night. Did my nephews see him getting shot? Did they see him lying there, bleeding? Did they try to run to their hurting father and/or uncle? My mind began to run rampant. Noah's daily routine would be to get David and Joseph, our sister Becky's sons, off to school and day care, go to work, pick the boys up, get them settled, feed them, bathe them, and get them ready for bed. Noah lived and breathed loyalty. He wanted to be there to make up for the time he missed, being gone for ten years.

Even though they were young, he knew the importance of having a male figure around and wanted to be sure he spent all the time he could with them. Noah would have sleepovers on the weekend with his kids, Scott and Tabatha; Derrick's daughter, Princess; and Becky's boys. They all would watch movies, have pillow fights, and prank each other. It was a family tradition to put mayonnaise or mustard on the first person to fall asleep at the sleepover.

Noah's patience was wearing thin, especially because he was getting into it with his children's mothers' of lack of time, money, and effort because he always had Becky's boys. Now he had started catching Becky in lies because his kids' mothers were telling him about her lack of responsibility because he was doing everything.

## Different

I arrived in Baltimore at midday on Sunday to be with my dad and sister after the murder. I was picked up from the airport by Jackie, to my surprise, who told me my father had overdosed and was at home resting, and that's why he didn't pick me up! On the ride from the airport, she explained, "Thank God the police were following the truck, because if they would have not stopped him, he could have died."

I was incredibly quiet in the car, paying attention to the highway exit signs. I remember seeing Exit 29B to Baltimore-Washington Parkway. I could picture Greenmount Avenue from North Avenue to Towson. I pictured myself standing where I was told my brother died.

Of course, when I saw my dad, he said he was fine, that they were overexaggerating.

"If I did OD, I would be in the ER right now."

As soon as we hit the city, I had Jackie take me around Greenmount. I walked from the corner where he was lying on Lorraine Avenue up Greenmount, through the 27th Street block, and I came out on the playground. I stood there in disbelief. I had so many memories flash before my eyes. I was crushed.

The next voice I heard was one of my brother's friends. He said, "Mecka, you need to go. Man, it's fucked up what happened, but Mecka you not safe out here." I was confused; this was my neighborhood. We grew up here. I began to cry. He said, "Mecka, I know, baby, but you gotta leave," and I did, angrily.

When I arrived at Nancy's house, everyone was in the basement. Nancy, her daughters, and a friend were going through my brother's things. I asked, "What are you doing?"

Nancy said, "Straightening up, so I can get this Christmas stuff organized."

I said to them, "Stop. I will go through my brother things. Get out the way!" I was upset that she and her daughter felt comfortable enough to think it was okay. Only Noah's father or one of his sisters should have done that. Our mother was deceased and our brother was in jail. The audacity of them!

Jackie was saying to Becky as they walked into the basement from the side door, "We need to do it for y'all father."

I stated, "I'm here for my father, not the drama and whatever else y'all trying to stir up." Scott and Tabatha's mothers dropped them off to me and they stayed with me while I was going through their dad's things. They were able to take everything they wanted of his: shoes, pants, shirts, and even a game system. I told them to take a comforter set—that way they had sheets and a cover of their dad's.

I found a key. I asked Nancy about it; however, her oldest daughter responded. "I know he has a box that it goes to. We didn't see it."

I was thinking to myself, *They were looking for something in my brother's things!* I gave them a death stare. I was pissed and they knew it. My dad walked into the room, along with Jackie and Bruce. My father was upset because once again Nancy had made it to where he could not help with the funeral. First his wife's, now his son's funeral.

Nancy went Christmas shopping for her daughters, granddaughter, and others before he got home on Saturday. Keep in mind, when my mom passed, she paid the bills, whereas my father could not help me with my mom's funeral expenses. From the look on my father's face, he was crushed, but I knew there was nothing I could say or do besides simply be there and try to make it as easy as possible.

Jackie let us know she and Bruce were going to cover the funeral. We needed to find a church; they had already selected the funeral home. Our mother's and father's sides of the family had not gotten along since we were children. I could see that Becky was making it a father-side and mother-side thing by saying, "Well, my mother's side is going to cook for the repast. They are going to do this, and they wanted this for Noah."

I was just trying to get it done. I did not feel we needed to rent a space for a repast, being as the two sides did not get along.

**A fire was burning in my belly....**

# Her Way

We were to meet at the funeral home after Jackie and I went to check out the church and ask about the repast prices. Even though I knew I was not staying at the repast, at least Becky would have a price. I did not want her to think I was trying to undermine her ideas or suggestions. By this time, Jackie had spoken to Patricia, who told Jackie she had given Becky some money to help with the repast. Once we arrived at the funeral home, Becky was already seated.

Now it was Jackie, Hope, Bruce, Becky, the funeral director, and me in the conference room of the funeral home. The first thing we discussed was the casket. They said it was eight thousand dollars. I said, "Like, for what? He will be cremated."

Becky responded, "I don't want my brother in a cheap-looking casket for cremation."

I said, "Mommie's casket did not look cheap, even though she was being cremated."

She said, "I want my brother to have the best."

*As if what I did for our mom was not good enough,* I was thinking, skin boiling inside. I wanted to speak on it, but I did not.

Keep in mind, she had been too busy to help me with any of the process for our mother. I bit my tongue and allowed the funeral director to finish.

He said, "That's the price for renting the casket. We will only remove the liner that your brother will be in from the casket and place the liner on a gurney to be cremated with your brother."

I was baffled! Clearly you could tell she had already known what she wanted, and I was to just agree, which I did because it was too much. She wanted family cars. I felt we did not need them; let everyone drive themselves.

Not only did she want a family car, but she wanted the Benz as a family car, and that is exactly what she got. At that point, I was just ready to go. Jackie asked her for the money Patricia had told her about.

Becky asked, "What, I can't go to the place?"

I ask, "What did you say?"

She repeated, "I'll go pay for it."

I told her, "Your aunt asked for the money because she is paying for the funeral. Why would you not give her the money?"

She responded rudely, saying I was just jealous and mad at her because nobody would listen to me and I wanted to be in control.

Yes, I was upset because our family knew who killed our brother, but no one was willing to say a thing. She allowed the story to run, insisting it was gang or drug related when we all knew that was not true and there was more to it. I was upset at the funeral home, thinking back to when I had to do it alone and she was too busy. We left the funeral home, everyone going their separate ways, giving us things to do and time to cool off. Aunt Hope gave Becky and me tasks to complete. We got pictures, poems for siblings and kids, and decided on a color to wear.

We were now at Nancy's, trying to get the obituary done. Aunt Hope, my father, and Jackie came in; Toya, Scott and I were already there.

Toya said, "Noah technically had three kids."

I jumped on her, saying, "I knew it. I knew it."

Unfortunately, Maddie had passed. Maddie was Noah and Toya's daughter. She was conceived after Noah came home; however, they were both seeing other people. The only ironic thing was that

Toya was seeing her current boyfriend the entire time Noah was in jail and never became pregnant.

Now, ten years later, her son's father was home. They stayed with each other, dealing with each other to give Scott special time with both parents. This went on for some time; however, Noah could not get past Toya dealing with her boy best friend after Noah was arrested.

Taking in the news of Maddie, Scott had a panic attack. I knew what it was; I had been having them since my mom passed. I believed he was having the attack because it became too much, sitting there looking at pictures of his father while we discussed the final arrangements.

We still called the ambulance because we all believed it could have been an asthma attack—Scott had severe asthma like his dad. The ambulance came, they cleared him, and I then had a talk with Scott about remaining calm and breathing. Scott, Tabatha, and I slept in Noah's bed—well, actually, our mother's bed. When he moved out of the house with Becky, he took our mother's bedroom set with him. I watched them as they slept. Surprisingly, they slept peacefully.

I went back upstairs and drank a little, which then turned into a lot of drinking. I lost the key to Noah's case. Days later, it was found.

However, still no sign of his box or money. My brother was the type to save money and stash it in his room somewhere. After going through Noah's things and listening to the conversations that had been going on, I now realized that my brother had been dealing again. I knew he would have money, drugs, and guns in his possession.

I wanted to find all of it, split the money between his kids, give the gun to law enforcement, and flush the drugs. By the time I arrived Sunday—Noah was shot Friday—the tiles in the walls around his room had been moved. I could tell someone knew my brother hid his money in the walls; we had the strangest way of hiding money, especially from ourselves. I dropped Scott and Tabatha off to their moms and went to my cousin Pam's house. I did not feel comfortable being at Nancy's house anymore.

While I was drunk, Nancy told me her daughter took a pair of shoes that my brother had sent to the house for someone else. That person had come looking for the package, and she had to get her daughter to bring it back. As I was sobering up, I could recall certain things that were said. Now I believe my brother was having sex with both of Nancy's daughters, and their reaction confirmed it. Wouldn't be his first time sexing sisters or mothers and daughters. I could only

shake my fucking head.

# Not Mentally Ready

I went to pick up Juanita, my mother's best friend. We did my hair and sat up talking all night at Pam's house. We did not even realize we talked all night now it was time for us to start getting dressed for the funeral.

We arrived at the funeral before everyone else, so I just walked around and stayed out of the way. I did not want anyone to say anything to me. After everyone in the family walked in, I came from the side and sat with Pam and Juanita, but not on the family side. I looked up and saw Cameron coming down the aisle. He did not look up. He sat about three rows ahead of me.

At this point my blood was boiling. He started to hyperventilate, and I wanted him to die right there. Aunt Shelia ran to get him an asthma pump and pumped it in his mouth for him. Soon after, Noah's true friends walked down to pay their respects and they saw Cameron. You could tell something was about to go down; however, I made eye contact with one of them. I was like, *No! Not here!* with my eyes, so they walked past him. A bullet could have hit me; I was right behind him. Cameron took a deep breath, a sigh of relief. The night Noah was shot, his mother took him to Philly for several days. No one saw Cameron until the funeral.

I had not seen David and Joseph the entire time I was in Baltimore. Becky uses her children as pawns to get people to do what she wants them to do and manipulate people in order to get or see them. When I saw my nephews at the funeral, I went over to see them while kissing and hugging Tabatha and Scott. Becky was trying to be smart and hold Joseph between her legs. I managed to take him from in between her legs. Once in my arms, he was shaking. You could tell he was afraid. I turned him away from his mother and he hugged me even tighter. I kissed him and let him know, "I am always here. It is okay. I promise that it is all right."

He said, "I'm scared, TeeTee."

I said, "I love you, Dank." (My nickname for Joseph.)

He replied, "I love you too, TeeTee."

At this time Bruce signaled me. It was time to shut the casket. My Dad could not do it, so it was up to Becky and me. I had brought a serenity prayer to put in there with him.

I said, "Come on Becky, let's read it together." She ignored me. I grabbed her hand and tried to console her while starting a second time at reading it among ourselves; it wasn't until Bruce yanked her arm, telling her, "Open your mouth" that she began—however, still mumbling. We shut the casket, and I went to give my dad a hug and a kiss and went back to my seat.

Becky and I were brought up twice during the funeral service over the microphone by clergy (first by Heidi, one of my mother's adult friends, then by Yonese, my cousin who only heard one side—Becky's side). I decided to leave. I was not going into my issue with anyone but my sister. I did not care how people viewed that. Without even waiting for the funeral to end, I went up to the front of the church, got a flower off the casket, kissed the casket, and walked out of the church.

Now the service was ending and people were making their way to the repast hall.

Donna my mom sister said, "Can I get a hug?"

I said, "You better get the fuck out of my face before I slap you. I been owed you one."

"In the name of Jesus," she responded. I walked past Becky and others after I attempted to stay and be seated, only to feel even more uncomfortable.

I was now at Pam's car, and all my cousins on my mother's side were outside. Cameron called my name. I ignored him. He came up to the window of Pam's car; I made no eye contact. He said my name two more times and eventually walked away from the car window.

Bruce then came up and said, "Mecka, your cousin wants to talk to you."

I told Bruce, "I have nothing to say."

Then cousin Mushan came up to the car said, "We all we got is family!"

I said, "This is not my family. I'm done." We pulled off. I was sweating. I felt like I was going to vomit in anger. My whole life, my mother raised us to stick up for each other, protect each other, and love each other. Noah did not receive that, even after serving ten years for one of his homeboys. He kept to the street code: no snitching. He lost precious time with his family for the streets. I was broken.

I went to Nancy's house because that was where my father was. I wanted to spend time with him before I left to go back to Atlanta. I was very happy when I walked in because Becky's sons were there. I had the pleasure of spending some one-on-one time with them. I could tell they were hurting, missing my brother and my mother, and they were confused. I was waiting for my plane ticket—my godfather Charles was working on it—while I just replayed the last eighteen months of my brother's life, especially because he was locked up for ten years, starting when I had to go to the jail in December with Aunt Hope to let him know our mother was gone. My dad was still on the road, and Becky could not take telling Noah. Her words. Keep in mind, years before she had gone to tell her boyfriend at the time that his grandmother had passed while he was incarcerated.

I had not been to a jail in over ten years. I was afraid. I thought back to the day I told my mom that I did not want to go to the jail to see my dad anymore. I did not like how the doors sounded when they locked, and I didn't like being patted down.

I was having severe anxiety, and God delegated the perfect angel to go with me. As each door shut (there were about fifteen of them), I felt my chest get tighter and tighter. When we finally got to the door, Noah was seated. He turned, looked around, stood up, removed his glasses, and dropped to the floor. The doors were opening, and we were able to go to him. We hugged him and kissed him briefly, but it felt long. Noah and I were very close growing up—

actually, nine months apart. I was his protector when he was ill from asthma, and he became everyone's protector after he realized exactly how strong he was.

He was crying. We were also crying. We just looked at each other.

He said, "What happened?"

I responded, "Mommie had a heart attack."

He quickly interrupted, "No, I heard all that. What happened to Mommie? She was simply fine!"

I said, "Noah, you know I am just telling you what's being told to me." He was very angry. He didn't know she had moved back to Baltimore, and he wanted to know why. I would not give him the answers. I told him, "Ask questions when you get home. You'll get the answers."

I told him that I was angry and hurt and felt simply lost and betrayed. I told him I needed him to come home to do what he needed to do, first for his kids and then for everyone else. When he asked about Becky, I just stopped. He did not like that. I told him, "I am not going to talk about her; she has a lot to learn, and I will not be her punching bag." We talked about a lot, but I told him, "I will not say bad things about her. Just get home and take care of you." I brought the kids back the next day, and it was an amazing visit.

## Just a Short Time Ago

While I reflected on my brother's life, I thought back to when my dad brought Noah to Atlanta (after I made sure he cleared it with his probation officer). He was like, "I'm coming. I don't care, they can't tell me no."

I said, "If they do, I'll be on the next plane up there." We enjoyed our time at Centennial Olympic Park, eating shrimp and grits, cleaning my backyard, trying to get my pool together, and Noah, Edward, and my dad partying. They were memories I will cherish. So will my daughters, hopefully his kids, and the other grands.

Flying for the first time for his niece's thirteenth birthday, he was cool as a fan. He admitted when got here that it was like I had said. He was nervous, but it was cool. He partied with Paris and her friends, getting her a whole other outfit for her party, and checked my dad. It was a night to remember. I thought about the conversations we would have when he just wanted to talk about life, reminiscing about Mommie.

I was thankful because up until Easter, I was able to talk to David and Joseph through Noah. He never told me what he and Becky actually went through. I assumed she was lying, taking his money, getting her hair done, eating out, going out, not paying bills, buying hair, all with him having the boys more than his children. Now I could no longer talk to them when I asked him to put them on. It was upsetting him a lot; however, he just wanted peace. He wanted to still be able to get them and spend time with them. I understood but did not agree!

Noah was not calling as much, and I knew why; however, he had promised that it would not happen. Little did I know, he had stopped calling because she did it to him. I am assuming he was crushed, confused, frustrated, and lonely. All the things I felt when I first realized how Becky truly was. He now had to go stay with my father's girlfriend at the time, because they were being evicted. She wasn't paying bills and was doing what she wanted with his money. Just as she did with me, her friends, Mommie, and Daddy. The only thing was that he was in shock. He needed my mom. He had come home, and now his back was against the wall, back to the streets.

Hearing this from Nancy when I came up for Pam's baby shower, my heart broke for him. Not only could he not tell me; he couldn't even look at me. He was incredibly sad. I just wanted him to know that I was there whenever he wanted to talk and that I knew the feeling. It hurt like hell. Now having to deal with the frustration of Becky without talking about her Noah called me scared and angry. Bruce my uncle, had put Noah NEW freedom at risk. Noah told Bruce he couldn't drive his car back from his lady house in the county because he didn't have a license. Bruce only thinking of himself assured Noah he would be fine because he was driving a cop car. Noah gets stopped because another officer realized it wasn't my uncle driving the car and suspected it was stolen. After Noah calmly explained to the officer he just came home from prison and stealing a car was not on his plans to do for his family. The officer called Bruce on his cellphone and my brother is free to go. Noah said "IN that moment it confirmed for him how they truly felt about him"

He had already felt the love for him was not matched as other male cousin as a young boy and teen playing Pop Warner football for Northwood. He loved playing however he didn't understand why we had to walk to and from practice when all our other cousins where driven. They would try to gift him with new gifts at Christmas and none for our brother and he wouldn't accept them. They didn't care to follow his case, to even help financially because in their eyes he was already guilty. Fact: HE DIDN'T SHOOT THE GUY. He believed had it been Jackie, Annette, or Bruce sons they would have had the best lawyer. Only to send a lawyer who mostly won his cases at the time for plea deals. My brother girlfriend was fitting that bill on her own. She was 1500 dollars short of complete payment and because of that my brother didn't go to trial.

Now he was gone.

I love you, baby. I'll never forget how you would lick my face if I told you to brush your teeth and I'd be stuck with that stench on my face but still laughing the whole time. When Edward does it, I think of you. Continue to watch over your kids and touch them ways only angels can…Kiss Mommie and Daddy for me!

TO BE CONTINUED………….

**God was preparing me from the beginning....**

I had the STRENGTH IN ME ALL ALONG....